# The FIRST FLEET

*A new beginning in an old land*

*Written and illustrated by John Nicholson*

ALLEN & UNWIN

Other books by John Nicholson
*Paper Chase: a Frantic Dash Around the World by Land, Sea and Air*
*Homemade Houses: Traditional Homes from Many Lands*
*Gold!: the Fascinating Story of Gold in Australia*
*Explorers of Australia*
*The Cruellest Place on Earth: Stories from Antarctica*
*Kimberley Warrior: the Story of Jandamarra*
*A Home among the Gum Trees: the Story of Australian Houses*
*Who's Running This Country?: Government in Australia*

First published in 1995 by
Allen & Unwin
9 Atchison St
St Leonards NSW 1590
Australia
Phone: (61 2) 8425 0100
Fax: (61 2) 9906 2218
E-mail: frontdesk@allen-unwin.com.au
Web: http://www.allen-unwin.com.au

10 9 8 7 6 5 4 3

National Library of Australia
Cataloguing-in-Publication entry:

Nicholson, John, 1950– .
    The First Fleet: a new beginning in an old land.

    Includes index.
    ISBN 1 86373 923 8 hb.
    ISBN 1 86448 017 3 pb.

    1. First Fleet, 1787-1788 – Juvenile literature. 2. Penal colonies – Great Britain – Juvenile literature.
    3. Penal colonies – New South Wales – Juvenile literature. 4. Convicts – New South Wales – Juvenile literature.
    5. New South Wales – Colonization – Juvenile literature. 6. New South Wales – History – 1788-1851 – Juvenile
    literature. 7. New South Wales – Discovery and exploration – British – Juvenile literature. I. Title.

994.402.

Designed and typeset by John Nicholson and Mark Carter, Melbourne
Printed in Hong Kong by Dah Hua Printing

# Contents

## Author's Note

History is partly a matter of fact and partly a matter of opinion. The events described in this book seem to have stirred up as many different opinions as there are people to write about them. There are even different versions of straightforward things like the amounts of food provided for the people of the First Fleet. I've tried to steer a middle course – and of course may have ended up satisfying no one!

I am grateful to Professor Alan Frost for his help and for the splendid lists in his book *Botany Bay Mirages,* to John Bendi at the Old Sydney Town, and to the many other authors and historians who have written on this subject.

# The Living Hell of Georgian England

Two hundred years ago few people in England lived happy and comfortable lives.

The rest faced a daily battle with hunger, violence, dirt and disease. Most city people lived in tumbledown tenements and hovels, crowded into dark, cluttered alleys. The streets were choked with rubbish and infested with rats. Raw sewage flowed along open gutters. There were no graveyards for the poor – large open pits called 'poor's holes' contained the rotting bodies of the dead.

Children went to work after their sixth birthday. Orphans (children whose parents were dead) and paupers (children from very poor families) were bought and sold for slave labour. They could be brutally punished for the smallest wrong-doings. Like all poor people they were often tempted to steal, in order to stay fed and clothed.

# Crime and Punishment

There was no central police force in eighteenth-century England, and crime was widespread. Most criminals were never caught, but those who were faced a range of bizarre punishments. The best they might hope for was a few days in the stocks or pillory. Perhaps the worst was to be chained to a staple in the local prison. Most prisons were damp, dark, smelly and crowded. Many were privately owned money-making businesses, and prisoners had to pay for their own food and bedding. Food scraps and sewage were left lying around the cells. Many prisoners died of starvation or the deadly epidemics which regularly swept through the prisons.

The death penalty was imposed for a

*Hulks like these housed prisoners awaiting transportation or labouring on harbour works*

large number of offences, not all of them serious by today's standards. Anyone convicted of 'impersonating an Egyptian', 'cutting down an ornamental shrub', or 'appearing on a highroad with a sooty face' could be hanged on the gallows! In fact, most people sentenced to death were pardoned by the King.

## Transportation

Another punishment was called transportation. Prisoners were sold to private contractors who shipped them to the English colonies in America. There they worked on plantations. The plantation owners had to release them after they had served their sentences.

Transportation seemed such a good idea. For the government, it got prisoners out of overcrowded jails. For the colonists, it provided labour. And it gave prisoners a chance to start life anew in healthy surroundings with some chance of 'making good'.

But in 1776 the scheme came to an abrupt halt. The American colonies rebelled, threw the English out and declared their independence. They wanted nothing more to do with the English, and especially they wanted no more English criminals forced on them.

This created an immediate problem – what to do with the convicts. For a while they were held in old navy ships, called hulks, anchored in estuaries near London, Plymouth and Portsmouth. The hulks were soon full to bursting and the government looked around for somewhere else to send the prisoners. The West Indies, Gibraltar, Newfoundland, Nova Scotia and various places in Africa were all considered. Finally Botany Bay, on the east coast of Australia, was chosen. The area had recently been explored by Captain James Cook.

## Why Australia?

There was more to this decision than just finding a good place to send wrong-doers. In the days of sailing ships, the timber for hulls, masts and yards and the flax to make ropes and sails were as vital to a great naval power like England as oil and steel are today.

Not far from Botany Bay lay Norfolk Island, and according to Captain Cook it was forested by tall straight pine trees, 60 metres high and ideal for ships' masts. On the ground beneath the trees, flax grew thickly.

The English were also looking for a base in the Pacific area, and they wanted to occupy Australia before the French got in.

So the grand scheme was born. The First Fleet would clear out the jails, provide a source of valuable shipbuilding materials and enlarge the British Empire, in one operation.

# The Ships of the First Fleet

In March 1787, 11 ships were assembling near Portsmouth in southern England.

Two were naval warships to guard the fleet against pirates and other navies and to keep an eye on the convicts themselves. Six were transports for the convicts, and three were storeships – all supplied by a shipping contractor, William Richards. The Navy ships would remain in New South Wales. The others would unload and then return to England, some via China to pick up cargoes. In addition to ships the contractor supplied sailors, and all the food, water and medicines for the convicts, soldiers and officials during the voyage. These chartered ships cost the government £49,486 – the largest single cost of the entire venture.

All 11 ships were built in England from oak, with masts of Baltic or North American pine and rope of Baltic flax and hemp. They were similar in design to Cook's *Endeavour*.

## The warships

SIRIUS, 531-tonne frigate (bottom left)
The flagship of the fleet was built in 1780-81. She was designed with a long flat deck to transport masts and spars from the Baltic Sea to British shipyards. She was renamed and given a complete refit for her new task. The *Sirius* carried 14 six-pound guns (they fired 2.7 kg cannon balls).

One of the last pieces of equipment taken on board by Captain Phillip was the chronometer used by Cook on his second and third voyages. A chronometer is a very accurate clock used for navigation.

SUPPLY, 170-tonne sloop (above)
A small ship described as an armed tender, she carried eight guns, but her main job was to carry extra supplies for the *Sirius*.

The transports (above, from left to right) were:
- *ALEXANDER – 452 tonnes, male convicts;*
- *SCARBOROUGH – 418 tonnes, male convicts;*
- *CHARLOTTE – 345 tonnes, male and female convicts;*
- *LADY PENRHYN – 338 tonnes, female convicts;*
- *PRINCE OF WALES – 333 tonnes,*
  *male and female convicts;*
- *FRIENDSHIP – 278 tonnes, male and female convicts.*

## The transports and storeships

Their average age was $2\frac{1}{2}$ years and they had been modified to carry convicts. Iron bars were fitted over the hatches; loop-holes were cut so that muskets could be fired at the convicts; and iron-spiked barricades were fitted to protect the upper decks.

The convicts were crammed into dark, unventilated holds. Each person had an area 1.8 metres long by 0.5 metres wide by only 1.3 metres high. They could not stand up. They could not see, because candles and lanterns were forbidden. They could not look out, because there were no portholes or

The storeships (above, from left to right) were:
- *FISHBURN – 378 tonnes;*
- *GOLDEN GROVE – 331 tonnes;*
- *BORROWDALE – 272 tonnes.*

windows. In calm weather they were allowed to exercise on deck, but in bad weather the hatches were battened down and the convicts lay in the dark, lapped by a heaving swill of seawater, vomit and sewage.

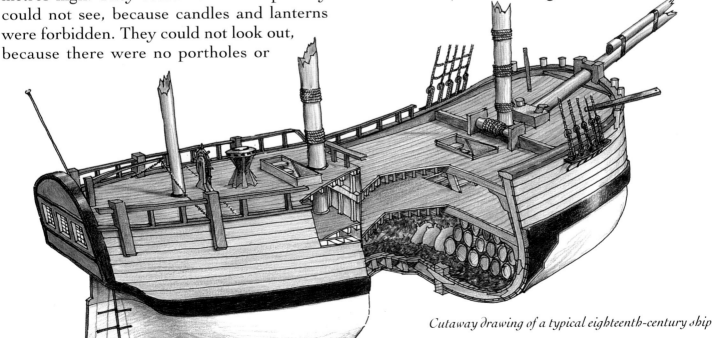

*Cutaway drawing of a typical eighteenth-century ship*

# The People of the First Fleet

On 6 January 1787, small boats began ferrying their cargoes of human misery from the hulks to the transports. As far as we know, there were 772 convicts jammed into the transport ships:

- 568 men
- 191 women
- 13 children

To guard the prisoners, sail the ships, and run the new colony there were:

- about 247 Royal Marines (soldiers)
- 210 Royal Navy sailors
- 233 merchant seaman
- 20 civil officers (lawyers, administrators, doctors, clergymen, etc.)

together with 27 wives and 19 children.

What sort of people were these unwilling pioneers?

## Captain Phillip

Captain Arthur Phillip was the man chosen to command the First Fleet and to govern the new colony.

His career as a naval officer had taken him to the West Indies, Brazil, India, and South Africa – all long and dangerous journeys. He had commanded large warships in battle, undertaken secret spying missions and was experienced in transporting convicts. Yet, at 48, he found himself on half pay and, not for the first time, out of work – until the job of leading the expedition to Botany Bay was offered to him.

He was brave, thorough, conscientious and even-tempered. He was also kind and fair. Later, when food was scarce in New South Wales, he ordered that all the colonists, from Governor to convicts, should eat the same rations. He was anxious also to treat the Aboriginal inhabitants of New South Wales with decency and respect, describing himself and the colonists as 'guests' of the Aborigines.

He was paid £500 a year for his difficult task.

*Sailors*                *Marines*                *Naval Officer*

## Major Ross

Major Robert Ross was the commander of the Royal Marines. He also became Lieutenant Governor on arrival in New South Wales. He was a bad-tempered, incompetent individual. Phillip got rid of him by sending him with a detachment of marines to settle Norfolk Island, 1600 km away.

## The Royal Marines

Like their commanding officer, Robert Ross, they were quarrelsome and lazy men, many of them failures in life. They refused to do the job they had been sent to do (guarding prisoners and supervising work parties), claiming that they were soldiers, not wardens. They must have made Phillip's life very difficult.

## The convicts

More than half of them were convicted of minor thefts: a loaf of bread or a shirt, for example. Perhaps they had had to steal to stay alive. They were the poorest of the poor in a harsh, disorganised society. Of the others, some were political prisoners, people who had spoken out against the injustices of society.

But many more were murderers, serious offenders and dangerous criminals, whose death sentences had been changed to transportation. Most were multiple offenders.

Among them were:
- 6 carpenters
- 5 weavers
- 2 butchers
- 1 fisherman
- 5 shoemakers
- 2 bricklayers
- 1 baker
- 1 gardener

About half the convicts described themselves as labourers. Only a few had skills or trades that would be useful to a young colony at the other end of the earth. To compensate for this, Phillip tried hard, before leaving England, to recruit more skilled people into the ships' crews. There were 16 ships' carpenters among the seamen.

Some of the convicts were very young. The youngest child was a chimney sweep, John Hudson. A criminal at nine, he was convicted of stealing a pistol and some clothes. Elizabeth Haywood, a 13-year-old clogmaker, was the youngest girl. She had stolen a linen gown and a silk bonnet and was sentenced to transportation for seven years.

*Convicts*

*Civil Officer*

# What Did They Bring?

Captain Phillip's fleet of 11 wooden sailing ships finally left England at 3 am on Sunday 13 May 1787. Over 25 000 kilometres of ocean lay ahead. Eight months later the First Fleeters would step ashore, into the complete unknown.

What would they need to take with them? What sort of food, and how much? What tools, equipment and building materials? What animals? What plants and what seeds? Going back to get something they had left behind would not be possible. They would have to make do, for at least two years, with what they had brought with them and whatever they could find on the spot.

## Food

They took enough food to last them two years (including the eight-month voyage). After this they hoped to be harvesting their own crops.

Each week, each of the officers, sailors and marines was allowed:

- 1.8 kg* dried salted beef
- 0.9 kg dried salted pork
- 1.1 litres dried peas
- 1.7 litres oatmeal
- 3.2 kg 'hard tack' or 'ship's biscuit'
- 400 g cheese
- 200 g butter
- 1/3 litre vinegar

(*In those days they didn't use kilograms and litres, they talked of pounds, ounces and pints – the quantities given here are equivalents.)

Pretty miserable fare, you may think! But spare a thought for the male convicts, who had to survive on only two-thirds of this ration. The woman convicts made do with just half of it!

Nonetheless, after just a few weeks at sea there was a lot of maggoty meat, weevily flour and mouldy cheese sitting in the hot stuffy holds of the storeships. Altogether there were:

- 138 tonnes of beef
- 69 tonnes of pork
- 88 000 litres of dried peas
- 132 000 litres of oatmeal
- 241 tonnes of flour
- 26 tonnes of cheese
- 22 000 litres of vinegar

## Clothing

Each female convict was allowed (for one year):

- 4 shifts (dresses)
- 3 cotton jackets
- 1 woollen jacket
- 2 canvas petticoats
- 2 'linsey-woolsey' (wool and cotton) petticoats
- 1 serge petticoat
- 3 handkerchiefs
- 2 caps
- 1 hat
- 4 pairs of socks
- 3 pairs of shoes

Male convicts were supposed to get:

- 2 jackets
- 4 pairs of woollen underwear
- 1 hat
- 3 shirts
- 4 pairs of socks
- 3 smocks
- 3 pairs of trousers
- 3 pairs of shoes
- No handkerchiefs!

Some of the uncomfortable-sounding women's clothing failed to show up. So when the fleet reached Rio de Janeiro, Captain Phillip bought 100 sacks of tapioca to add to the food rations. The unfortunate women convicts, now in rags and tatters, were given the empty sacks to make clothes.

## Tools and equipment

At the far end of the earth, the convicts would need to start completely from scratch: building houses, clearing the land and growing their own food. They brought with them a bewildering array of hardware:

- 700 spades
- 700 shovels
- 2100 hoes
- 700 axes (plus 700 spare handles)
- 747 000 nails
- 10 sets of coopers' (barrel-makers') tools
- 40 mills
- 40 wheelbarrows
- 12 ploughs
- 30 grindstones for sharpening tools
- 6 carts
- 4 timber-carriages (sets of wheels for transporting logs)
- 14 fishing nets
- 80 carpenters' axes
- 20 shipwrights' adzes
- 700 hatchets

*Cooper's hammer*

*Hatchet*

*Gimlet*

*Auger*

*Padlock*

- 175 claw hammers
- 175 hand saws
- 140 augers for drilling big holes in wood
- 700 gimlets for making small holes in wood
- 504 saw files for sharpening saws
- 300 chisels
- 6 butchers' knives
- 30 pairs of pincers
- 100 measuring tapes
- 50 pickaxes with 50 spare handles
- 5 sets of blacksmiths' bellows
- 10 forges for metalwork and horseshoes
- 20 pit saws (see p.23)
- 700 clasp knives
- 50 hay forks
- 42 splitting wedges
  - 8000 fish hooks
  - 576 fishing lines
  - 36 masons' chisels
  - 12 brick moulds (see p. 23)
  - harness for 6 horses and 12 oxen
  - 6 harpoons for killing whales
  - 12 lances for killing whales
  - 48 sets of candle-making equipment
  - 6 bullet moulds
  - 9 sets of flax-processing equipment
- 18 coils of whale line
- 2 millstones for grinding wheat and barley into flour
- 1 loom for weaving canvas

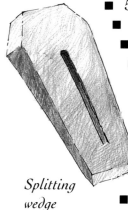
*Splitting wedge*

Some of the quantities seem strange. Why were there so few (six) butchers' knives, for example, and so many spades, shovels and hoes? The organisers of the expedition obviously did not expect much fresh meat to be eaten, but they certainly expected much planting and tending of crops.

Building would mainly use local materials, but some ready-made items were included:
- 5448 squares of glass
- 10 000 bricks
- 200 hinges
- 60 padlocks
- 26 marquees for married officers

And domestic items were not forgotten:
- 330 iron pots
- 700 wooden bowls
- 700 wooden plates
- 500 tin plates
- 40 camp kettles
- 36 candlesticks
- 3 candle snuffers
- 5040 candles
- 44 tonnes of tallow (animal fat) for making more candles
- 38 kg of sewing twine
- 24 spinning wheels
- 800 sets of bedding for the convicts (soldiers' and sailors' bedding would have been included in their own kits)
- 1524 combs
- 84 razors
- 100 pairs of scissors
- 1 bible and 1 prayer book

## Arms and ammunition

The First Fleet was a military operation. It faced many possible dangers, both from the Aboriginal people whose land was being invaded, and from other colonial powers greedy (like Britain) to add yet more territory to their empires. So Phillip made sure that he had plenty of firepower on board. Heavy guns, handspikes, hand grenades, muskets, blunderbusses, 900 cannonballs and 500 kg of small shot and buckshot all went along.

There were also dozens of mysterious items with obscure names like 'cook's patent sponges with rammer heads', 'wadhooks', 'lintocks with cocks', 'wandmill tilts', 'men's harness', 'budge barrels', 'hambro line' and many, many more!

## Seeds and plants

There were no handy gardening guides to tell settlers what would or would not grow in New South Wales, so they ended up taking everything they could think of. For any particular fruit or vegetable, a number of different varieties was included, just in case.

## What they left behind

All in all, the First Fleet seems to have been remarkably well equipped. However, some very important things were left behind:

- some of the clothing for the woman convicts, as we've already seen;
- certain building materials – some lime to make mortar and a small amount of good-quality timber for doors and window frames, for example, would have been enormously useful;
- all the tools necessary to maintain the muskets;
- and, worst of all, the ammunition for the marines' muskets! – a terrible omission. When Phillip found out he kept it a close secret for fear of mutiny on the transports. Some musket balls were obtained in Rio de Janeiro, but not enough. Later, when food was scarce, hunting of wild animals for food was restricted by this shortage of ammunition.

Food was not forgotten, of course, but there wasn't enough. For several years, before successful crops were grown, the new colony lived on the edge of starvation.

# The Journey

Fine weather meant smooth sailing on the first leg of the journey. They reached the island of Tenerife on 3 June. On 5 August the fleet sailed into Rio de Janeiro, where it stayed for a whole month. The sick were taken ashore, extra stores were bought, and boatloads of oranges were distributed daily to prevent scurvy.

By mid-October the fleet was in Cape Town, and they spent another month replenishing stores, repairing ships, and buying large numbers of live animals. Loaded now to capacity, the ships embarked on the last and longest leg of the journey. The further they sailed from Cape Town, the colder and stormier the weather became, and the lower people's spirits fell.

Their arrival at Botany Bay on 20 January 1788 can have done little to lift those spirits. The bay was shallow and poorly sheltered. The surrounding country was flat, with sandy soil, a few stunted trees and little fresh water.

Over the next few days they searched the coast for a better spot and they made their first contact with the Aboriginal inhabitants who told them to *warra* (go away). Later they were astonished to see two large European ships enter the bay. The French had arrived. Phillip avoided hostilities with these colonial rivals and headed north for Port Jackson where he selected a site with running water and a good deep anchorage.

They called it Sydney Cove.

# The Other End of the Earth

### 26 January 1788

The anchors rattled out, the officers shouted orders and the ship's crews furled their sails. The oppressive heat of a midsummer's day beat down on the newcomers as they viewed their surroundings in uneasy silence.

At length a boat was lowered and Lieutenant William Collins went ashore with a small group of convicts. They cleared a patch of ground and hoisted the British flag, the Union Jack.

As the day wore on, the quiet wooded cove became a frenzy of activity. Stores were unloaded, trees and undergrowth were cleared, tents pitched, cooking fires started and a blacksmith's forge set up.

### 27 January

Most of the male convicts were landed and started work. Some immediately escaped and headed for Botany Bay, but the French brought them back. (Later, a convict family stole a small boat and sailed all the way to Timor, 5000 kilometres away. Most of the convicts who tried to escape were not so lucky – they either died in the attempt or came back.)

### 28 January

Most male convicts and some animals were landed.

### 29 January

Most animals came ashore, along with Phillip's prefabricated timber and canvas house.

## 30 January

Phillip's own animals were landed, the first plants went into the ground, and convicts started building a storehouse.

## 1 February

A party of convicts under Henry Dodd started clearing land at Farm Cove (now part of the Sydney Botanic Gardens). They planted vegetables and salad greens. After a week, all the marines' tents, civil officers' tents, hospital and laboratory tents had been pitched. Phillip's 'house' was up, many plants were in the ground and some of the convicts had tents. The rest improvised shelters from sheets of canvas (mainly old sails) brought for the purpose, bark, tree branches and whatever else they could find.

## 6 February

The female prisoners were taken off the ships and allotted to tents and huts on the shore. The process took all day and, as evening fell, a mighty thunderstorm struck. Flashes of lighting and sheets of rain seemed to release all the pent-up frustrations of the journey. Prisoners, sailors and marines all got horribly drunk and a night of passion and violence followed.

## 7 February

Everyone assembled, the band played, the marines marched. There was a short ceremony and Governor Phillip scolded the convicts for their unruly behaviour. A holiday was declared and the officers sat down to a celebration lunch of cold, maggoty mutton.

# The Iora People

For 30 000 years before the arrival of the First Fleet, the Sydney Cove area had been home to Aboriginal people. For the Iora, life was rich in story-telling, music and ceremonies. The many sandstone caves provided dry, secure homes and there was good fishing in the sheltered bays at Port Jackson and Pittwater. The Iora fished from bark canoes using fish hooks made from shells, lines made of bark fibre and spears. They also gathered oysters and other shell-fish. With spears, stone axes and fire they hunted for animals in the open forests of redgum, scribbly gum and angophora trees, and in the moist gullies dense with cabbage-tree palms and she-oaks. They were probably healthier and better-fed than most Europeans at the time...that is, until 26 January 1788.

Soon the newcomers were competing with the Iora for food, particularly for fish. Convicts began stealing the Iora people's fishing lines and spears. Later, European diseases like cholera and influenza swept through the starving tribes, killing many people. Small-pox, another killer disease which arrived about the same time, probably came from Asia through Aboriginal people in northern Australia.

Governor Phillip tried hard to make friends with the Aborigines. At first, however, they showed little interest. Later they became angry as the invasion started to affect them. Upset by the worsening stand-off between whites and blacks, Phillip eventually captured some Iora men and tried to persuade them of his good intentions. It was a funny way to try and make friends, but one of them, Bennelong, was soon on good terms with Phillip, who built a house for him at Bennelong Point. Phillip took him back to England, together with another Iora man, Yemmerrawannie, who died while he was there. Bennelong returned later to Australia.

Why did the British government occupy this country when it must have been obvious that the place was already someone else's home?

Many European countries at the time expanded their empires by invading and taking control of land belonging to less powerful people in America, Africa, Asia or the Pacific. One excuse was the genuine belief that no one could claim ownership of land unless they farmed it by growing crops or grazing animals on it. Aborigines weren't farming Australia in this way, so the British just sailed in and took over.

If it happened today we would all be furious, and most Aboriginal Australians still regard the white people as invaders.

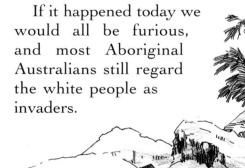

# First Buildings

The tents and improvised shelters put up during the first days ashore were adequate in fine weather. Later, with winter coming on, some more permanent structures would be needed. The 16 ships' carpenters began building huts for the marines.

They ran into problems straight away. Sydney Cove was well wooded with tall hardwood trees – so hard in fact, that axes and saws soon blunted or broke. To clear the area they resorted to gunpowder and blew trees out of the ground! And hard and strong as the timber was, it proved useless for building purposes, because it shrank, twisted and split within weeks of cutting. Later, in the nearby valleys, they found cabbage-tree palms whose timber was easily sawn and chiselled or split for roofing shingles. The cabbage trees were all used in just a few months, so they started on the she-oaks, which also provided good building timber.

A midshipman called Henry Brewer, who had had some experience in an architect's office, designed a simple single-roomed dwelling. Many one-roomed huts like this were built in the first few years.

## Brewer's simple cottage design

Roof thatched with reeds cut from Rushcutters and other nearby bays

Thatching was placed on battens which were the waste bits from milling

Rafters were unsawn saplings

Thick mud fireplaces were built on sandstone hearths. Chimneys were like the walls, except with a thicker layer of mud inside

'Wattle and daub' walls: the whole frame was covered inside and outside with mud, applied with a spade and then smoothed with a trowel. Finally a thin coat of pipeclay (abundant in the nearby tidal flats) or limewash (made from burning oyster shells collected by women convicts) kept the rain out

Windows had no glass, just a wattle-stick lattice

Sawn top 'plate' fixed to top of posts

150 mm x 150 mm corner posts were set 900 mm into the ground and grooved to house the ends of thin wattle sticks. Smaller posts, every 900 mm were also set into the ground and grooved. Walls were about 2.1 metres high

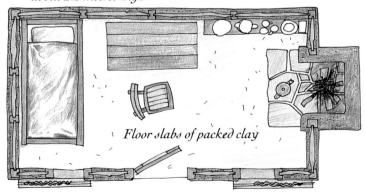

Floor slabs of packed clay

## Better buildings

The early buildings did not last well. Rain washed away the mud. Almost every week a thatched roof would catch fire. Many of them simply collapsed in heavy rain. Improvements were needed.

Roofs were made of timber shingles, split from cabbage-tree or she-oak timber. They were fixed to the battens with wooden pegs. Making the pegs was another job for the women convicts

Posts were still set in the ground at the corners

The top plates were now grooved.

A ground plate or bottom plate, also grooved, was laid on the ground

Vertical slabs of wood made up the walls, their top and bottom ends inserted in the grooved plates. Cracks were filled with mud

Door with leather hinges, 1.8 metres (or less) high

Drop-log construction
Another variation in which substantial logs with tapered ends were dropped in between grooved posts. Cracks between the logs were filled with mud

## Pit sawing

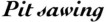

Without the luxury of today's timber mills, the early settlers used unsawn timber (logs or straight saplings) whenever possible. Squared or sawn timber could only be produced by pit sawing, an arduous job involving two men, one working in a deep hole in the ground. The log to be cut was placed on rollers (small logs) and manoeuvred into position over the pit with the help of wedges and levers. The two men, one on each end of a long saw, then slowly sawed the log up into planks. The man above, called the top-notcher, had the heavier but more skilled work. The one in the pit got a lot of sawdust in his eyes!

Chimneys were now brick or stone. The local stone was soft and easily cut

## Brickmaking

In April 1788, good clay for brickmaking was discovered. One convict, James Bloodsworth, was a brickmaker by trade and brickmaking equipment had been brought along. Sydney's first bricks were made using a quick and rough version of traditional English methods.

Convicts pounded the clay into a coarse powder with logs, using natural depressions in rock, like a large mortar and pestle. Water was added, and bare-legged convicts stamped around in the sticky mess, which was left to stand for three days before being used.

The mould was wetted and dusted with sand to prevent clay sticking to it (like butter and flour in a cake tin), then placed over the stock ready for the clay to be pressed in. The mould could then be slid off, leaving the wet brick sitting on the stock. The bricks were sun-dried for three days and then fired in a kiln. The first bricks were used to build a house for the Governor.

Stock

23

## Dawes' Observatory

In addition to its many other tasks, the First Fleet had a program of scientific work to follow. Marine Lieutenant William Dawes, the officer responsible for engineering works, had a wide interest in science. He was given the task of constructing an observatory and using it to view the stars of Australia's night sky, including an anticipated visit by a comet. The building would also be Australia's first weather station.

A site for the building was chosen on 17 March 1788 (see map pp. 26-7). Working with three marines and four convicts, Dawes had his observatory finished in just four months.

The delicate scientific instruments were mounted on top of a large solid rock about 1.8 metres high. The building was built against, and partly over, this rock.

Dawes used the drop-log method of construction (see p. 23), with she-oak timber for the wall posts, panels, rafters and shingles. Governor Phillip must have thought this an important project because some of the settlement's precious nails were allocated to the job.

The octagonal observatory room had a revolving roof, supported probably on cannon balls, to allow all parts of the night sky to be viewed. Removable roof panels were made of canvas painted with white lead-based paint.

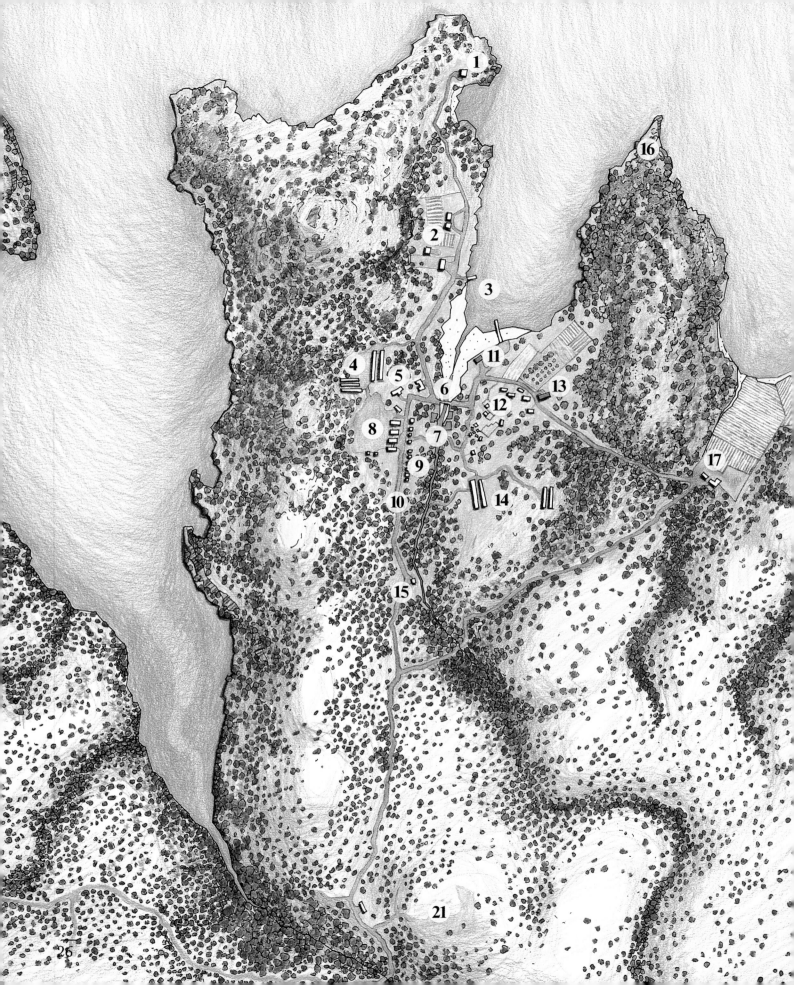

# The first settlement

1 Within a few months Lieutenant William Dawes had built a small stone observatory at Point Maskelyne (now Dawes Point)

2 During the first year a timber hospital, 25 m by 7 m, was built and a vegetable garden was planted for the patients. Nearby another garden provided vegetables for the crew of the *Supply*.

3 The first wharves

4 The male convicts pitched tents in a little valley between Grosvenor and Essex Streets

5 The first church, a 22 m by $4^1/_2$ m wattle and daub structure, was started in July 1793

6 Five months after their arrival, Phillip put the convicts to work building a timber bridge

7 Later, convicts hacked water tanks out of the sandstone banks of the stream, near what is now Hamilton Street. The first, finished in 1792 held 40 000 litres. Tank Stream very soon became polluted with animal and human waste

8 Marine barracks and parade ground

9 The marine officers' tents (later brick houses with shingled roofs) were arranged along the west bank of the tank stream. Each officer had 0.8 hectares of land to garden

10 At first called High Street, then Sergeant-Major's Row, George Street was not part of Phillip's grand plan for Sydney. It just happened – as a rough bullock track along the most convenient route

11 Store. Log walls and a canvas roof protected the first vital stores

12 Civil officers' houses

13 Governor's house. Phillip brought a prefabricated timber and canvas house with him. It was 13.7 m by 5.3 m and had five windows. He did not endure its discomforts for long. The first bricks manufactured were used to build a solid two-storey Government House. An area of $2^1/_2$ hectares was cleared and planted with fruit trees and vegetables

14 Female convicts' and some male convicts' (e.g. tradesmen's) tents.

15 Gallows

16 Phillip decided to unload all the livestock at Cattle Point, later called Bennelong Point because of the 4-metre square timber hut Phillip had built there for his Aboriginal friend

17 Farm Cove. Food was the new colony's first priority. On 1 February, a group of convicts under Henry Dodd began clearing land there. By September there were $2^1/_2$ hectares of wheat, 3 hectares of barley and $2^1/_2$ hectares of other grains

18 Garden Island is now attached to the mainland, but in 1788 it was separated by 300 metres of water. The crew of the *Sirius* used it as a vegetable garden secure against human and animal thieves

19 The first huts were thatched with rushes, gathered at Rushcutters Bay and other bays.

20 Pinchgut Island, now Fort Denison, was used as a prison

21 Brickfields. Good clay was found on a steep hill about a kilometre south of the town, so brickmaking operations were set up there. This area was an important ceremonial ground for the Iora people who held regular corroborees there

# Hunger and Anarchy 1788-92

With a few basic buildings up, the colonists settled in to face their first winter...and their first major problems. They realised straight away that the soil at Sydney Cove was not very good for growing things. Their first crops withered and died, or failed to grow at all. Cattle, sheep and pigs (those that had survived the voyage) escaped into the bush or ate poisonous grasses and died. Fish numbers in the harbour dwindled. Many people became ill, leaving fewer hands for the farming and building work.

Days turned into weeks, weeks into months and months into years as all eyes turned daily to the sea, searching for the ships that never came. One ship, the *Guardian*, her holds filled with food for the colony, struck an iceberg and sank after leaving Cape Town. In April 1790 rations were cut to 1 kg of salt pork, 1.8 kg flour and 0.75 l of rice per week. The Second Fleet, carrying some food but more convicts, arrived in June 1790, making matters worse.

The lazy and unco-operative attitude of the marines led to an increase in stealing (particularly of food). The colony subsided rapidly into anarchy.

Governor Phillip told all the colonists that they must take responsibility for feeding themselves. Each person or family was given land to grow vegetables and allocated an area of the harbour for fishing. He also restored law and order by appointing groups of responsible convicts to patrol the village.

## Parramatta

In December 1788 a farm was begun on better land at Parramatta, further up the harbour. Henry Dodd, who came with Phillip as his personal assistant, was one of only a few experienced farmers in the colony. He was put in charge of 12 hectares and was soon producing good crops of maize, wheat, barley, oats and potatoes.

Lieutenant Dawes surveyed (mapped out) a town, and a new Government House was built at Parramatta.

## Children

Forty-five children arrived in New South Wales with the First Fleet. By the middle of 1790, 83 new babies had been born but a total of 25 children had died. This seems like a lot, but in London at that time only one in two children survived to adulthood.

In 1789 the first school was established by Isabella Rosson, a convict who had previously been a teacher, She taught the children of convicts and soldiers to read and write, to add up and subtract. In 1791 another school was opened by Mary Johnson at Parramatta.

The children of the colony endured several years of hunger and discomfort – but they probably grew up healthier, happier and with a brighter future than they would have in England.

## Phillip goes home

On 11 December 1792 Governor Phillip left Sydney to return home. He was tired, sick and disappointed with the colony's poor progress. But his achievements in the face of severe difficulties were enormous. There were now 700 huts in Sydney, as well as some substantial houses, a hospital, observatory, jetties, a dockyard, government stores, Governor's house and a windmill.

Food crops were now thriving. On government land alone there were:

475 hectares of maize
83 hectares of wheat
10 hectares of barley
48 hectares of vegetables

Many people had vegetable gardens and orchards. The colony was now almost self-sufficient – its most difficult years were over.

# Glossary

**adze** heavy tool for cutting away the surface of wood

**battens** thin strips of wood usually supporting a roof

**bellows** simple pump for sending a jet of air into a fire to make it burn better

**blunderbuss** short, trumpet-shaped gun firing a spray of pellets

**brig** two-masted, square-rigged vessel with additional fore-and-aft sails

**buckshot** small pellets, many of which are fired at once from a gun

**chisel** small, sharp-ended tool for shaping wood or stone

**convict** person found to be guilty of a crime

**estuary** area of water where a river flows into the sea

**flagship** the ship carrying an admiral in command of a fleet of ships

**flax** a plant with long narrow leaves, used for making rope, linen and linseed oil

**forge** (or smithy) a fireplace with bellows used for melting and shaping metal

**frigate** a small warship

**gallows** a structure for hanging criminals

**gimlet** a small tool for making holes

**grindstone** rough revolving stone for sharpening metal tools

**handspike** wood and iron lever, used by sailors and heavy gun crews

**hatch** trapdoor covering an opening in the deck of a ship

**hatchet** light, short-handled axe

**hardwood** wood from deciduous trees (trees that lose their leaves)

**hemp** a plant used for making rope

**hoe** tool for loosening soil

**hold** large area inside a ship where the cargo is carried

**hulks** old warships used as prisons in eighteenth-century England

**Iora** Aboriginal inhabitants of the Sydney region

**lime** a white powder made by burning seashells or limestone and used in mortar for bricklaying. Also used as a fertiliser to help plants grow

**limewash** white paint made from lime and water

**loom** machine for weaving fabric out of yarn or thread

**marines** soldiers based on warships

**marquee** large tent

**mason** person who cuts and shapes stone, and builds stone structures

**musket** light gun used by soldiers before rifles were invented

**navigation** methods of working out a ship's position using geometry and the stars

**observatory** building containing telescopes used for watching the stars, weather or wild animals

**pillory** wooden frame with holes for head and hands, used for punishment of offenders

**pincers** tool for gripping small objects

**pipeclay** a fine white clay used to make tobacco pipes, and for other purposes

**pit-saw** long saw used by two people to cut logs up into planks

**plough** large piece of machinery used on a farm for loosening soil and cutting furrows. Usually pulled by horses in the eighteenth century

**rafters** sloping beams supporting a roof

**shingles** roofing tiles made from split timber

**smock** protective outer garment like a large shirt or a dress, worn for working

**sloop** small one-masted vessel with a mainsail and a jib

**spar** long, strong, straight and round piece of timber used for a ship's mast or yard

**spinning-whorl** a small wheel steadying the motion of a spindle wheel (part of a spinning wheel for making yarn)

**staple** U-shaped piece of iron, firmly set into a wall, onto which prisoners were chained

**stocks** wooden frame with holes for the ankles and sometimes the wrists, used for punishment of offenders

**storeship** ship carrying supplies of food and equipment

**tapioca** hard, white, grainy food from the cassava plant, used to make a rather boring pudding

**tender** small vessel or vehicle accompanying a larger one to provide supplies or other help

**tenement** building containing several rented homes or flats

**thatched roof** roof made of straw or reeds

**top plate** flat piece of wood along the top of a wall

**transport** ship carrying large numbers of people

**transportation** punishment of convicts by taking them to another part of the world where they are forced to work

**wattle-and-daub** a method of building walls. Wet mud is plastered over a light framework of sticks

**yard** horizontal pole holding either the top or the bottom edge of a ship's sail

# Index